SHRI RAMA, THE UNIVERSAL IDEAL!!

By: Dr (Er) Om Prakash

Professor

Abstract

Blessed aspirants! May the grace of Shri Ramachandra be with you all! In this paper, the learning from Ramayana has been illuminated and its relevance to virtuous management has been advocated. Lord Shri Rama lived human life in the most practical way possible in its different aspects of social relationships firmly established in the Dharma, through His well-regulated personality and highly refined conduct. An ideal life, whether corporate or personal, can be lived on earth by following the guidance of this glorious leader of humanity, the true representative of the Supreme Divinity who manifested himself for the benefit of all subsequent generations. The Ramayana teaches one to lead a true life as it helps one to practice and spread the virtues that adorned the person of Shri Rama. The teachings of Ramayana help one to rise beyond himself or herself and tune mind accordingly. The descent of the grace of the teachings of Ramayana potentially helps one to rise from a mere manager to a transformational leader. This transformation can really be achieved through the teachings. In Ramayana, there is a striking panorama of hope and despair, sacred idealism and worldly delusion, sacrifice and desolation, attack of weakness and tragedy, magnanimous dedication to virtue and humble devotion, steadfastness and fortitude, triumph over the evil and glory of victory.

Keywords Ramayana, Shri Ramachandra, Transformational Leadership, Dharma, Adharma, Universal Ideal

Introduction

Shri Rama, the ideal of goodness, mercy, benevolence and divine life on earth, was revealed to destroy the forces of Adharma, to protect and establish Dharma, to personally live the canons of Dharma and thus become an example of life -- perfect and par excellence for all mankind. The Ramayana, the celebrated story of Shri Rama, lists in its first chapter the glorious characteristics of Shri Ramachandra, whom the eminent sage Narada declares as the supreme jewel among the people. Rama's Name, His form and His conduct have been the object of constant remembrance, contemplation and emulation by people for centuries.The word "Rama" is interpreted in the Ramarahasyopanishad as the combination of the essence of the Narayana-Ashta-Akshara and the Shiva-Pañcha-Akshara, that is, "RA" and "MA", without which, the Ashtakshara and the Pañchakshara not only would they not have the proper meaning but they would have the opposite (Sri Swami Sivananda, 2017). The Rama-Nama is also considered as the essence of the thousand Names of the Lord. It is the Taraka Mantra, the "ship" that makes the mortals cross Samsara or death. The power of the Name is well understood when it is known that even the wrong pronunciation turned the delinquent Ratnakara into the sage Valmiki. Shri Rama is an object of meditation because he is the Avatar of Lord Vishnu, the Preserver of the universe. Shri Rama incarnated when the five planets were on their ascendance. The unique planetary condition suggests the glory of Shri Rama's life (Sri Swami Sivananda, 2017). The Dharma that one finds in Him is the best refuge. Read the Ramayana and you will understand the greatness of Shri Rama, the true Arya Purusha, the ideal son, the ideal brother, the ideal husband, the ideal king. Shri Rama lived human life in the most practical way possible, as a whole in its different aspects of social relationships firmly established in the Dharma, through His well-regulated personality and highly refined conduct. An ideal life can be lived on earth by following the guidance of this glorious leader of humanity, the true representative of the Supreme Divinity who manifested himself for the benefit of all subsequent generations (Sen, 2005).

Universal Ideal of Shri Ram: A symbol of unity beyond borders

Lord Rama of Ayodhya is nothing but a symbol of a universal bond that transcends religious, caste, creed, sect, modes of worship, province, language and the boundaries of countries and continents. His profound influence transcends these distinctions, making him a symbol of unity for the entire human race. He serves as a bridge between diverse cultures and beliefs, uniting humanity through his exemplary conduct and ideas that have endured through the cycles of ages. We have read that the headlines feature familiar figures such as Prime Minister Narendra Modi being named in Time magazine's 100 most influential people, Ashwin being recognised as ICC's Person of the Week and the enduring dominance of Nadal and Djokovic in tennis. However, amid these contemporary stories, transcending the cycle of decades, centuries and eras, emerges a timeless hero, from the beginning of his life to the end, the true hero is undoubtedly Lord Ramachandra of Ayodhya.

Lord Ramachandra has continuously won the hearts of all by playing the role of an ideal son, husband, brother, male friend, friend, ruler, guide, leader, philosopher, warrior and father. His influence transcends not only religious boundaries, but also the boundaries of caste, creed, sect, ways of worship, province, language and even countries and continents. This character serves as a role model for the entire human race, surpassing the stature of great men of any religion or country on earth. Lord Ramachandra, who connected not only the Indian subcontinent but the entire world with his conduct and thoughts, stands as a symbol of the unity of mankind.

The Valmiki Ramayana, composed in Sanskrit by Maharshi Valmiki two thousand years ago, is the oldest and original version. While Valmiki's rendition is widely recognised, the Ramayana exists in 309 different versions, written in different languages and styles. This epic tale has been expressed through various literary forms such as poetry, epics, oya, unbroken hymns, lyric poetry, stories, novels, dramas, paintings, crafts, dances and folklore, including the art of shahiri. It is noteworthy that the number of Rama Kathas expressed through these forms reaches crores. In Indian languages, apart from Sanskrit, there are 11 Ramayanas in Hindi, 8 in Marathi, 25 in Bengali, 12 in Tamil, 12 in Telugu and 8 in Oriya. In addition, Ramayanas have been written in Gujarati, Malayalam, Kannada, Assamese, Bhojpuri, Urdu and their respective dialects. The story of Ram has been the most written and discussed tale globally.

Respected for his pure thoughts and conduct

Rama stands as an eternal ideal worshipped by every generation for ages. Universally worshipped as the seventh incarnation of Lord Vishnu and the first incarnation of God in human form. This exalted position has been given to him not only because he is an incarnation of God but also because of his sattvic thinking and behaviour. Rama was a revolutionary who protected the forest dwellers during his exile and taught them the Vedas. Rama, who united with the forest men like monkeys, bears, Nishads, Matangas and taught the evil Ravana a lesson, is a similar 'Samarasathayogi' (symbol of equality), from an ideal son who obeys his father to a sensitive son who dispels the suspicious half-baked mentality of his subjects.

Even though such an ideal character of a benevolent king has been drawn in Valmiki Ramayana and this Ram Katha should not be considered fictitious. If we consider such Ram to be true and worship him as a deity. In many Ramayanas or Ram Kathas, the character of Ram has been portrayed in different ways. While studying these Ram Kathas, we come across many interesting things.

Various images of Rama

Mention of Rama and other characters of Ramayana can be found in the oldest Vedic literature, Atharva Veda (19-39-9) and Rig Veda (1-126-4). The Shatapatha Brahmana text (10-6-1-2) also introduces these characters. The Valmiki Ramayana, consisting of seven sections and 24 thousand verses, emphasizes the human existence of Rama, while the Adhyatma Ramayana presents his character from a divine perspective. Maharishi Vasishta edited the discourse of Rama in the Vasishta Ramayana, which mentions twelve names and explains twelve roles of Rama. The Ananda Ramayana depicts the last phase of Rama's life, and in the Mahabharata, Maharshi Vyasa recited the Ramopakhyan during the Aranyaka Parva (forest festival).

Rama is mentioned in the Drona Parva and Shanti Parva of the Mahabharata, his character is portrayed as ideal due to the influence of Valmiki Ramayana. Sanskrit plays, including Bhasa's Pratima Nataka and Bhavabhuti's Uttararamacharita, present sentimental and fanciful perspectives on the image of Rama. Various Sanskrit scholars and playwrights, such as Kalidasa, Bhatta, Pravarasena, Kshemendra, Rajasekhara, Kumaradasa, Vishwanatha, Somadeva, Quality Data, Narada and Lomesh, consistently paint a similar picture of Rama as a gentleman and an ideal person.

Rama Katha in Jataka Tales

The narrative of the Rama story is narrated in the Buddhist tradition through three Jataka tales, known as the Dasharatha Jataka, the Anamaka Jataka and the Dasharatha Katha, each of which is different from the Valmiki Ramayana. In the Dasharatha Jataka, Rama and Sita are portrayed not as husband and wife, but as brother and sister, highlighting the unique interpretation of the Rama story in Buddhism.

The Jain tradition presents its own version with the Padma Purana in Sanskrit, the Vimalasurikrit Paumachariu in Prakrit and the Svayambhukrit Paumachariu, where Padma is believed to be the original name of Rama, who is considered the greatest of the 63 Shalakas (great men) after the Tirthankaras. However, in Jainism, Rama is not considered an incarnation of Vishnu. Emphasizing non-violence, the Jain tradition states that Lakshmana killed Ravana to make his Shalakapurusha Rama non-violent.

Sikh Guru Gobind Singh depicted Rama as an aggressive warrior in his tale Ramavatara, while Mughal emperor Akbar translated the Ramayana into Persian while retaining the essence of Valmiki's original. The Persian

Ramayana, which contains 176 illustrations by artists such as Basawan, Keshavlal and Miskeen, largely matches Valmiki's narrative.

Ramacharitamanas

Goswami saint Tulsidas' epic work, Tulsi Ramayana, takes the character of Rama to new heights, emphasising every human being's devotion to Rama. Ramcharitmanas appears to have been written with this very purpose in mind, reinforcing the call for individuals to become devotees of Rama. Various regional adaptations, including the Champu Ramayana by Parmar Bhoja, Vishnudas's Ramayana in Gujarati, Bilanka Ramayana by Sharladas in Oriya, Torave Ramayana in Kannada, Assamese Ramayana, Bhavartha Ramayana by Sant Eknath Maharaj in Marathi, Gadima's Geetaramayana, Rama Avtaar in Kashmiri and Ramacharitram in Malayalam, all consistently portray Rama as an ideal person. In the Tamil Kamban Ramayana, Rama is held guilty for incidents like Agnipariksha (fire test) and Sita's exile, which are absent in the Ramcharitmanas. Samarth Ramdas Swami emphasizes the ideal form of Rama for 'balopasana' (resilience) and national liberation, while Rashtrasant Tukdoji Maharaj employs Ramcharitra for village development. Swami Karpatri has presented a scientific interpretation of the Rama Katha in his book Ramayana Mimansa, and talented poets like Maithilisharan Gupt have integrated Rama into poetry by portraying him as a companion.

Different nations believe in Ram

From India's neighboring countries to the small country of Central America, Peru, the story of Ram has reached here. People there have accepted it with faith and have tried to adopt the ideals of Ram in their conduct. There is Tibetan Ramayana in Tibet, Khotani Ramayana in East Turkistan, Kakabin Ramayana in Indonesia, Seratram, Sairiram, Ramkeling, Patniramakatha in Java, Ramkirti (Ramkirti) in Indochina, Khmer Ramayana, Yutoki Ram Yajna in Burma, Ramakien in Thailand, Bhanubhaktiya Ramayana in Sanskrit language in Nepal, Ramayana in Arabic in Malaysia, Ramayana in the form of Maharadiya Lawana in the Philippines, Janakiharan Ramayana in Sinhalese language in Sri Lanka...etc.

The story of Rama has left a lasting impact across all countries and languages. In Sri Lanka, Hanuman and Sita have a greater influence than Rama. In the Tibetan Ramayana, Sita is portrayed as Ravana's daughter, and in

Laos, the Ramakatha takes two different forms. In the Philippines, the names of the characters in the Ramakatha have changed, Rama to Mandiri, Lakshmana to Mangavarna, and Sita to Malai, also known as Tihaiya. According to this version of the Rama story, Ravana is considered evil, yet he is not killed by Rama. In the Brahma story Rama is depicted as a Bodhisattva, and in the Japanese Rama story, Sambo-i-Kotaba, the golden deer is removed. Ravana becomes a yogi, wins Rama's heart and abducts Sita in Rama's absence, Ravana is depicted as a dragon or serpent.

The lasting influence of the Rama story is evident in many countries globally. Cities such as Ramavati Nagar and the Amarpur Viharaya temple are dedicated to Rama, Lakshmana, Sita and Hanuman. In Thailand, places such as Ajudhiya (Ayodhya), Lavapuri and Janakpur along the Sarayu River in Java reflect the widespread influence of the Rama story.

Thailand continues the tradition of ruling with padukas like Bharata and taking oath by reciting shlokas like Rama during Vibhishana's coronation. Rama is considered the first ruler in China and the Rama-Ravana war is depicted on the Angkor Wat temple in Cambodia. Lines from Valmiki's Ramayana are inscribed in every temple in Java, and the kings of Peru claim to be descendants of Kaushalya Sutra. In Malaysia, every Muslim person adopts one of the names Rama, Lakshmana or Sita as a prefix, which is an example of how Lord Ram Raya has played an important role in breaking the barriers of language and religion. Ram, the pinnacle of literature, also appears in various forms of folk art. From Ramlila in Uttar Pradesh to Dashavatara in Konkan, Kathakali dance in Kerala, the pictorial style of the Mithila region in Bihar and the elaborate depiction of the entire Ram Katha on the Hazararama temple of Vijayanagara-Hampi. Ram's presence is alive in various cultural expressions.

Rama is revered through various artistic forms, including the Rama Kathan (Vari Liba) performed by forest-dwelling tribes such as the Bhils, Gonds, Khasi, Bodos, and the singing of the Rama Powada, known as 'Pena Sakpa'. The notion that Rama, the essence of all beings, has passed away evokes both wonder and contemplation. The research of Belgian-born Christian priest Father Kamil Bulke, who received the first Hindi doctorate with a thesis on 'Ram Katha-Origin and Development', along with the archaeological findings of Dr. Ram Avtar, explored more than two hundred places, The Ramayana period cements the character of Rama. Despite the variations in the portrayal of Rama in various Ramayanas, Rama's image as an ideal and gentleman remains impeccable. Carrying Rama in one's heart and recognising the presence of Rama in every individual can pave the way to eliminate discrimination and treat every individual as a human being. With such awareness, the revival of Ram Rajya is no longer impossible.

Lord Rama: Shri Ram inspires the society to have higher ideals

From the point of view of public welfare, Ramrajya is known as an ideal and complete system. Mahatma Gandhi had wished for a similar system of governance for modern India, which is in line with Ramrajya. There is a unique amalgamation of monarchy and democracy in the character of Ram. Shri Ram's name is associated with Maryada Purushottam because he always followed the rules. He was a great king, ideal son, high class disciple, ideal brother and husband, who will be remembered in this form till eternity. Shri Ram walked on the path of truth, religion, mercy and dignity throughout his life. This is why his rule was called 'Ram Rajya'. Everyone expects that 'if the son is like Ram', 'if the king is like Ram', 'if the character is like Ram'.

From the point of view of public welfare, Ramrajya is known as an ideal and complete system. Mahatma Gandhi had wished for such a system of governance for modern India, which is in line with Ramrajya. There is a unique amalgamation of monarchy and democracy in the character of Ram. He did not become king by being elected through voting, but he did not do anything without knowing the wishes of the people. He never ignored the wishes of the people for his own selfish interests. Keeping this ideal in mind, Ram abandoned his beloved wife Sita, and fulfilled the responsibility of a king even after suffering personal hardships. Ram was never impatient to grab the throne, so the weaknesses of the throne could not bind him. He did not go around selling assurances. He did what he said. He had the unwavering trust of not only his subjects but also his family. He was deeply seated in everyone's hearts. He was free to do as he pleased, but he always remained bound by the decorum of the state rules.

After 14 years of exile, Ram was getting the throne. But he did not become impatient and unrestrained. He was least concerned about himself. First of all, Ram ordered his servants to make his friends like Sugreeva take a bath. After this, Ram called Bharat and untangled his matted locks with his own hands. After getting the throne, not only the people but also the gods praised Ram. Vedas and Lord Shiva also prayed to the Lord. Ram got so much respect, but he did not become proud of it and lose his wisdom. He remembered his duty. As soon as Mahadev left, the first thing that Lord did after getting free time was to arrange good accommodation for his friends who had come from Lanka. This was Ram's first order as a king. Lord first became concerned about the care of those who had faith only in Ram. Usually, after getting the throne, the king becomes more anxious about himself, he worries about a beautiful residence for himself. But Ram did not have the nature to think about himself.

After becoming the king, Ram paid attention to his subjects and established a welfare state. Everyone started living within their limits. Ram established coordination between humans, animals and nature. Humans became virtuous, animals controlled their animal instincts and nature became ever-thriving. Due to the absence of pollution in society, there was no problem of pollution in nature. Everyone's life was simple and balanced. No one had enmity with anyone. All the inequalities have come to an end due to Ram's glory.

Ram did not do any magic to end these disparities. Ram achieved this by adopting the policy of cooperation, consultation and coordination. He gained respect for himself by respecting everyone. He believed in taking decisions with everyone's cooperation. He was in favour of coordination, he did not want to create separation or discrimination by any of his conduct. Ram explains human ideals in a very clear manner and says that the greatest religion is to work for the welfare of others. In fact, this is a unique principle to limit human life. If you do good to others, you will surely be benefited! One who quenches the thirst of others cannot die of thirst himself. But one who keeps others thirsty is more likely to die in agony. There can be no greater meanness than tormenting others. Man was saved from this meanness in Ram Rajya. He should avoid it in every era. One may get momentary happiness by causing pain to others, but mental satisfaction cannot be obtained.

As a king, Ram inspires the entire society to have high ideals through his good conduct. Ram's character is not double-faced. He never wished to shed tears for his subjects on stage and enjoy himself at home. As a king, his life was completely dedicated to his subjects. He believed from his heart that everyone gets a human body by great fortune and it should be used properly. The king should make such arrangements that every person can develop himself to the fullest. By saying this, Ram wants to incline his subjects towards high ideals. He has made such arrangements in the kingdom where a man can live a life of comfort and convenience according to his profession; and he also wants that his subjects should attain salvation by behaving well. This concern of Ram is an essential duty of a great king. A king who does not care about the arrangements for the complete development of his subjects cannot get the love of his subjects. His system of governance cannot provide peace and happiness to the society. Ram knew this truth very well. That is why he created a practical system to improve the worldly and spiritual life of his subjects. That is why even today everyone wishes for Ram Rajya.

The concept of the welfare state, which we keep hearing about, has also been given to us by Ram. The foundation of Ram Raj is that the government stands with the deprived, the exploited and the needy. He advocates the economic policy of collecting more taxes from the rich and helping the poor. Today's governments also say the same. The most convenient words in current politics are 'Dalit Adivasi'. Ram is the first patron of the manifestation of the innate talent of this class. The reign of the King of Awadh was spread across India. If he wanted, he could have fought with Ravana with his royal army. He could have taken help from other kings as well. But Ram preferred to fight with Ravana and other demons with the forest dwellers and their inherent strategic strength. We can also give Ram the credit of forming the first royal army with forest dwellers and Dalits.

The life of Maryada Purushottam Shri Ram, his devotion to duty and high ideals are the source of guidance and inspiration for the entire humanity. Maryada Purushottam Shri Ram exists in the hearts of every person as an ideal. In fact, Shri Ram is the eternal basis of India's consciousness. Just like butter is contained in curd. The last point to which Ram inspires people is also the real indestructible power of Ram. We should inculcate the ideals of Shri Ram in our lives and play our role in creating a better society and an environment of mutual harmony. Where there is a means of development and progress for everyone.

Ethics: Follow the Path of Righteousness

The noblest lesson in the Ramayana is the supreme importance of virtue in the life of every human being. Virtue is the spiritual spark of life. The cultivation of virtue is the process of unfolding the latent divinity in man. The glorious incarnation of the supreme Truth, Shri Ramachandra, has set the example through His own life of how to follow the path of virtue. May humanity follow in His footsteps and practice the ideals that He valued, for only in this way can there be lasting peace, prosperity and well-being in this world in general and the corporate world in particular. No one but the virtuous can be truly happy. It cannot be said that someone lives with dignity except the one who has the correct sense of duty and the will to implement it. One must be imbued with a definite conviction about the supremacy of moral principles, ethical values, and spiritual ideals that should guide one's daily actions and serve as a powerful means for the cultivation of human personality (Sri Swami Sivananda, 2020). That is the purpose of life. That is the way to the purpose of the modern virtuous and prosperous Company (MUNIAPAN, 2007). An example of a successful company is the one that does what promotes harmony, goodwill and peace, and does not do what inspires the opposite effect. Do what is universally considered good, fair and appropriate, what is sure to produce positive effects, and do not do what generates negative results. That is the judgment criterion. This is how one should decide between right and wrong. Another example of a successful company is its virtue of being credible and not deviating from the path of truth. This is the very basis of a company that works ethically and considers the welfare of its employees (MUNIAPAN, 2007). A successful manager would one who eliminates what produces a negative reaction in others and reinforces what quickly generates a sense of well-being in him and others as well. But, at the same time does not get carried away by the euphoria of doing well and being good. It is not something special that is expected of you. It is your duty. The only way you can make tomorrow a better day is to think and do today what will lead to better tomorrow. Have an open heart and mind, but accept only what is good, appropriate, and worth remembering. Try to correct in yourself first what you dislike in others. Accept only what is good in others and ignore the rest. Your own happiness depends on how you conduct yourself. Don't complain about the circumstances. Try to make the best of everything. Spiritual aspirants, reflect, brood, analyze and reason about what should be the aspiration you should have and what not, what you should do and what you should abstain from. Think correctly. Speak sweetly and truthfully. Act honestly, fairly, and selflessly. Grow, evolve and improve like this every day, every moment. THE RAMAYANA HERO Lord Rama, the hero of the Ramayana is the Purushavatara of the Supreme Being who incarnated as the son of King Dasaratha of Ayodhya. He was the joy of his mother Kausalya and the very life of Dasaratha. True to the Lord's Purushavatara, Shri Rama's qualities of heart and head exemplified the summary of human perfection that man can achieve in life. His body was made of iron. His heart was tender and charming. His mind was flexible. Even as a child, he acquired such skill in archery that there were none to match him in firing arrows lightning fast and hitting the target unerringly (Sen, 2005). This is confirmed by Lord Krishna's statement in the Bhagavad Gita, when He explained His countless aspects to Arjuna, the Pandava prince: "Ramah Shastrabhritamaham- I am Shri Rama in the handling of arrows". Although born and raised in an atmosphere of pleasure and fulfillment appropriate to his royal heritage, he cultivated great simplicity and Vairagya, which showed the philosophical bent of his mind and detachment from the ephemeral objects of the world. He was a "Jitendriya" who expressed, in every sense, a resolute mind and perfect control over the senses. However, he had a heart to feel for others in their sufferings and misfortunes, and he did everything possible to relieve them of their grief. Shri Rama fully translated into his own life the teachings of the Upanishads: "Matri Devo Bhava, Pitri Devo Bhava, Acharya Devo Bhava and Atithi Devo Bhava", fulfilling his duty towards his parents, showing great devotion to his Guru and providing hospitality and kindness to those in need. Note his bravery when, as a fifteen-year-old boy, he accompanied sage Visvamitra to the forest. He showed great courage by killing the two Rakshasas, Maricha and Subahu for the sole purpose of protecting the Dharma. Note his respect in the court of King Janaka when he raised the bow and broke it as proof to receive Sita's hand in marriage (Sen, 2005). Cultivate the qualities of selflessness and sacrifice that he displayed in fulfilling the wishes of his stepmother Kaikeyi by renouncing the kingdom and going to the forest in exile for fourteen years without the slightest feeling of offense or ill will towards anyone, much less towards Kaikeyi. The glory of renunciation, "Tyagenaike Amritatvamanasuh," as the Upanishads declare, is manifested in this act of Shri Rama. Observe once again Shri Rama's egalitarian view of friends and foes when he gave shelter to Vibhishana, knowing full well that Vibhishana had come to him from Ravana, the king of Lanka who was his staunch enemy, thus establishing his " Sharanagata Vatsalatva - quality of giving refuge to those who take refuge in him ". Note their true friendship by fulfilling the promise he gave Sugriva, the king of the monkeys, to install him as king of Kishkindha after killing his brother Vali and that when he himself was in trouble, thus maintaining his composure even in adverse circumstances (Gombrich, 2005). Observe his cosmic love when he performed the last rites on Jatayu, the king of birds, who died from the wounds that Ravana inflicted on him with his saber when he tried to rescue Sita from the king of demons. A fact that is indicative of Rama's feeling of unity of all souls. Notice his kindness and magnanimity in giving Ravana three days of time on the battlefield, asking him to make up his mind to return Sita, even then, thus showing his willingness to forget and forgive all that has happened. Finally, notice his detached feelings even towards Sita for whom he had to go through many trials and tribulations in life. After the coronation, following his successful return from Lanka, he discovered that his beloved wife could not face criticism and public scandal, not because he did not trust her chastity but simply in the interests of the majority. Such was the glory of Shri Rama, the light of the Ikshvakus race. May God bless humanity to absorb the virtues of Shri Rama and put them into practice in their own lives, particularly in this iron age in which the Dharma has receded (Losty, 2008).

THE IDEAL OF THE SUPREME DUTY

Lord Rama is man's supreme ideal of Dharma, submission and discipline. He shone more for the adornment of his virtues than for his royal garb. His great personality and His blameless life of supreme dignity, compassion and righteousness are a perennial inspiration for humanity at all times. The kingdom of Rama has become immortal as a state par excellence, based on the ethical conduct of life. The secret of the glory of the kingdom of Rama was the conception of duty that dominated all other factors. The people of the time, from the highest, the Rama monarch, to the most humble and lowest, and the last of the citizens were governed by a sense of duty in every aspect of life, private or public. The Ramayana is imbued with this unique spirit. In this ideal Dharma, that could be observed in the golden age of the solar dynasty, Raghuvamsha, the most inspiring was that fervent desire to fulfill one's moral obligations and one's own duty, at any cost, in the interests of the Dharma and human welfare (Gombrich, 2005). As defender of the faith and protector of the saints,

Dasaratha's subtle sense of duty caused him to put aside all consideration and send the two young princes, Rama and Lakshmana, to protect the Yajna from the Rishis in the Dandakaranya. The reaction of Queen Sumitra to Lakshmana's decision to follow Rama to the forest is full of that glorious concept of the supreme duty. Forgetting herself, she said, "O son, Lakshmana, consider Rama as your father Dasaratha, Janaki as myself (your mother), and the forest as the city of Ayodhya. Go son, go happily to the forest " (Sen, 2005). And what did Lord Rama do? He put aside obligations to his loving mother, his brothers and the loving citizens of Ayodhya. Rama felt that at that time a son's greatest duty was to uphold his father's honor in the name of Truth and the cause of Dharma. His loyalty to this ideal was unconditional and foolproof. The divine Prince turned his back on the pleasures of the palace and the throne, and chose the dangers and hardships of the forest. Because He chose the path of duty, that is, He responded to the call of higher duty. Until the end we find this sublime ideal of duty and self-sacrifice. Rather than offend the conception of righteousness and virtue in the least of His subjects, The great king chose to inflict upon Himself the greatest torment and to put the noble Sita through the agonizing ordeal of separation and desolation in the jungle. Didn't Lakshmana have a duty towards noble

Sita? He surely had it and was aware of it as well. But with the greatest pain he saw that the greatest duty was to obey his older brother and carry out his orders as king and ruler, who he knew was the embodiment of virtue and Dharma. The greatest and most moving manifestation of this great Ramayana ideal is the immortal Jatayu's offering of himself on the altar of supreme duty. He was in an uneven fight with the mighty Ravana. Jatayu could very well have avoided the conflict. It had nothing to do with Sita. He was not bound by any particular obligation. But Jatayu had risen from the soil of Bharatavarsha, from the depths of whose mother's heart rises the glorious maxim, "Paropakaaram Idam Shareeram" - this body is really meant to help others. The noble and courageous Jatayu responded to this unspoken call for this supreme duty of man - the duty to help others, to serve others, to control the Adharma, and to succor those who are in distress. This is the true life. This is the heroic life. Let faith fill you with strength to live such a life of adherence to supreme duty. May the Name of the Lord give you the power of self-sacrifice in the cause of the supreme Dharma. May the glorious example of the Ramayana ideal inspire all of you with soul force to lead a Divine Life of self-denial, sacrifice and service to all! Be brave in the fulfillment of Dharma and duty. Worship the ideal of Rama. Become like Him through a unique devotion to Him. May His Divine Grace lift you through Paropakara to the Parama-Dharma of the supreme Kaivalya Moksha! Om Shri Ramaya Namah! The Rule of Law The rule of law, which all democratic governments cherish, was the ideal of Rama Rajya. It was a formal ideal and, although in some respects highly puritan, did not lose sight of realism. He paid attention to the practical aspect and still defended some of the finer principles of government and of individual and social ethics. His concept of international relations was remarkably modern. Persuasion was attempted first and then the Vibhishana episode took place. Lanka was invaded, but it did not become a peripheral province of the Ayodhya kingdom. After the purpose of the war was accomplished, the people were set free under the rule of their own king. It was a magnanimous gesture and highly moralistic in its ideal. Only very democratic governments will be able to meet such an ideal even if it is not in such a short period (Pathak, Singh & Anshul, 2016). Ideal government The welfare of the subjects was the main consideration of the ruler. Nothing else mattered, not even the king's personal interests. The king's first duty was to see that the people were happy and content, that there was justice and the rule of law, that human considerations were not hampered by social distinctions, and that, above all, public opinion was allowed to exercise its full influence. Even in such remote times, it was understood that the best government is the one that governs the least. It is surprising to note that Shri Rama went to such an extreme of giving up his pregnant wife and banishing her to a hermitage, being that she was the queen and first lady of the kingdom, and all for the sake of what we could call today a symbolic opinion. But this indicates, above all, the way in which a ruler must conform to a strict standard of living and rigid personal conduct, not only as he would consider it ideal but as his subjects expect of him. Shri Rama's personal life and happiness were indeed secondary to the inflexible rules that governed his imperial life. It is extraordinary and surprising that such an ancient Indian kingdom has harbored and practiced such a meticulous sense of property and that its rulers have voluntarily submitted to it (Pathak, Singh & Anshul, 2016). Keep the lessons in mind Shri Rama's devotion to the ideal of monogamy, his refusal to marry again after leaving Sita, was truly magnificent, especially in a time when polygamy in the upper class was more the rule than the exception. There are numerous such lessons in the Ramayana. We also have the beautifully honest and selfless example of Urmila, Lakshmana's wife, to whom Valmiki does not pay much attention. Could a modern wife allow her husband to go into exile, voluntarily, for fourteen long years immediately after marriage, regardless of her personal interests and wishes, and only because of his sentimental attachment to his brother? Every page of this great book has a lesson in humanity. If modern man paid attention to at least some of them and if he had the determination, the courage and the strength to put them into practice, life on earth would be much better, happier, more peaceful, meaningful and justified (Losty, 2008).

Conclusion:

The RAMAYANA Lesson If something justifies life, it is the law of virtue. Virtue is not just a part of a moral code; It is the basic principle that sustains the purpose of life, makes one fulfill his responsibility as a unit of society, affirms the dignity of the human being and the dedication of man to the ideals of truth and justice, elevates him from everything whatever is vulgar, mean, bad or unfair. The Ramayana lesson is a perfect ideal for everyone. Simple yet glorious, normal and yet rarely followed, fundamentally human and still an agent of spiritual conversion. It is an ideal that has had a determining influence on the design of the structure of Hindu society and has always been an inspiring example worthy of emulation for all who are loyal to it (Pathak, Singh & Anshul, 2016).

References

Gombrich, R. F. (Ed.). (2005). Ramayana Book Four: Kishkindha (Vol. 4). NYU Press. Losty, J. P. (2008). The Ramayana: Love and Valour in India's Great Epic. British Library. MUNIAPAN, D. B. (2007) VALMIKI RAMAYANA AND ITS RELEVANCE FOR TRANSFORMATIONAL LEADERSHIP. Pathak, P., Singh, S., & Anshul, A. (2016). Modern Management Lessons from Ramayana. PURUSHARTHA-A journal of Management, Ethics and Spirituality, 9(1), 52-56. Sen, A. (2005). Ramayana: Book 1: Boyhood (Vol. 1). NYU Press. Sri Swami Sivananda (2017). Hindu Gods and Goddesses. Retrieved from https://www.dlshq.org/religions/rama2.htm Sri Swami Sivananda (2020). Significance of Ramnavami. Retrieved from

http://sivanandaonline.org/newsupdates/significance-of-ra mnavami/

www.ingramcontent.com/pod-product-compliance
Lightning Source LLC
Chambersburg PA
CBHW031255130726
47988CB00008B/3357